YOUR KNOWLEDGE HAS VALUE

- We will publish your bachelor's and master's thesis, essays and papers

- Your own eBook and book - sold worldwide in all relevant shops

- Earn money with each sale

Upload your text at www.GRIN.com
and publish for free

Bibliographic information published by the German National Library:

The German National Library lists this publication in the National Bibliography; detailed bibliographic data are available on the Internet at http://dnb.dnb.de .

This book is copyright material and must not be copied, reproduced, transferred, distributed, leased, licensed or publicly performed or used in any way except as specifically permitted in writing by the publishers, as allowed under the terms and conditions under which it was purchased or as strictly permitted by applicable copyright law. Any unauthorized distribution or use of this text may be a direct infringement of the author s and publisher s rights and those responsible may be liable in law accordingly.

Imprint:

Copyright © 2015 GRIN Verlag
Print and binding: Books on Demand GmbH, Norderstedt Germany
ISBN: 9783668665736

This book at GRIN:

https://www.grin.com/document/416993

Abbe Marten

The Progression of an American Urban Government

GRIN Verlag

GRIN - Your knowledge has value

Since its foundation in 1998, GRIN has specialized in publishing academic texts by students, college teachers and other academics as e-book and printed book. The website www.grin.com is an ideal platform for presenting term papers, final papers, scientific essays, dissertations and specialist books.

Visit us on the internet:

http://www.grin.com/

http://www.facebook.com/grincom

http://www.twitter.com/grin_com

During the Revolutionary War, the thirteen colonies that made up America did not have a central government and were only just forming independent state government. Through the first and second Constitutional Congress', America united in its resistance against Great Britain and adopted policies to abolish English authority over the colonies. This Continental Congress called for the colonies to form their own independent governments and they appointed five men to a committee to draft the declaration of independence. On July 4, 1776 the Constitutional Congress adopted the declaration of Independence which proclaimed the independence of America from the crown. However, now that the United States was a free nation, how should the new government be set up?

This 18th century conflict separated the nation into two distinct groups: the Federalists and the Anti-federalists. The Federalists, who were led by Alexander Hamilton, were those in favor of a stronger federal government and advocated for the ratification of the constitution, a system of checks and balances, a strong executive branch of government, and saw no need for a bill of rights. This group was made up of wealthy businessmen from the North who supported the commerce and industry of America. However, on the other side were the Anti-federalists, led by Thomas Jefferson, who favored the idea of a stronger state government with the Legislative Branch holding more power than the Executive Branch. Jefferson was in support of a decentralized agrarian republic that included efficient organization. While Hamilton feared anarchy and stressed the importance of order of society, Jefferson feared tyranny and stressed the importance of freedom.

With the draft of the constitution, the Federalists felt that it was structured well enough to prevent tyranny of the Executive Branch and thus no Bill of Rights was needed. This group claimed that the separation of the governmental powers into three independent branches of the government would protect the rights of the people in the nation. Because each branch represented a different aspect of society and since all of these branches are equal, no one group in the United States could gain control over any other group. In addition, the Federalists felt that a formal Bill of Rights listing specific rights guaranteed to all Americans was a dangerous thing. It would be impossible to list all of the rights on a document so that the federal government wouldn't violate any, so instead of only drafting a partial listing, there should be no list at all. The Federalists published these viewpoints and arguments to the Anti-federalist's concerns in The Federalist Papers.

The Anti-Federalists were against the ratification of the Constitution because they believed that if gave the federal government too much power. This group was made up of farmers, debtors, and other lower class people of the rural and southern areas of the nation whom were loyal to their state governments. They argued that the Constitution gave an excess amount of power to the national government at the cost of the state governments. They felt that both the executive branch and the congress held too much power. The Anti-Federalists believed that as Americans, they had just gained a myriad of rights now that they were free from England and a Bill of Rights was necessary for the new national government to be stopped from taking these rights away.

Thanks to the Federalist Papers, the Federalists were able to break down some resistance from the Anti-Federalists and win enough support from their opponents so as to win ratification of the Constitution. The first states to ratify this document, Delaware, Pennsylvania, and New Jersey, ratified it in 1787 and in June 1788, New Hampshire became the ninth state to ratify the Constitution which met the requirements for the United States to adopt the Constitution so it would go into effect. However, some states, especially New York, was deeply against the ratification of the Constitution for fear that it would transfer civil liberties away from the people and instead to an authoritarian government. In return for their support, the Federalists promised that a document outlining civil liberties would be added to the Constitution by the Congress, the Bill of Rights. With the convening of the new Congress, guided by James Madison, a Bill of Rights was carefully drafted with amendments addressing specific individual freedoms that were written specifically to appeal to the House and Senate so as to win approval. Some of the rights included: freedom of religion, press, speech, and assembly, the right to bear arms, the right to trial by jury and due process, protection against cruel and unusual punishment etc. These issues and several others were covered in the first ten amendments now known as the Bill of Rights. Finally, in December of 1791, the Bill of Rights was approved and went into effect thus assuring liberties for all free white men in the country.

During the industrialization of the United States, culminating during the period of 1870 to 1900, urban governments faced unprecedented issues that cities had never faced before. Due to both migration and immigration that created an urban population that was both ethnically and racially stratified, cities had begun the process of rapid industrialization, commercial expansion, and technological changes that redefined the social structure and economic relationships of the United States. The cities faced problems such as overcrowding, ill health, poverty, and crime due to the cities having to too rapidly expand to accommodate all of the newcomers into the urban setting. The existing government of the United States and municipal governments of the cities that had evolved in the urbanization of the early nineteen century did not have a remedy for these problems and instead seemed to "generate political chaos". Before 1850, most mayors could only exert a limited amount of control over municipal policy however this was soon to change as the urban cities began to dominate America.

As the industrial era brought changes in transportation, banking, communications, and technology, the political atmosphere of the urban cities broadened and developed rapidly. Voting rights expanded to those outside of the elite class and new political involvement opportunities were opened for those of the poor and working classes. Local politics were reshaped based on the racial and ethnic stratification that dominated the city and by the 1870s, "the machine" began to dominate and shape politics in these diverse urban cities. These machines were political associations that differed from the current established government agencies. The political bosses acted as brokers for economic and political interests, creating a centralized authority that dominated the fragmentation of power within the existing government.

Despite the political bosses of this era being depicted as corrupt dictators, most notably boss Tweed of Tammany Hall, in fact they acted more as executives of networks of smaller bosses. Big-city machines were brokers of the smaller machines that were organized at the ward level. Bosses controlled this hierarchy through the support of others, with monetary donations streaming in through the big bosses and back through a reciprocal flowing of material benefits that was distributed to those loyal to the bosses and their cities. This money that was generated came also from forms of graft, both "honest graft" involving investment capitalism and dishonest graft involving criminal activity. The basis of the political machines was located in taverns and saloons, where the working class congregated and could personally become involved with the urban bosses through conversation and banter. Most of these big city bosses were immigrants themselves or second-generation immigrants whom knew the plight of the poor and working classes in the cities firsthand; since they were able to identify with these people, the bosses became the first form of welfare in the city. Those immigrant voters who supported the political machines saw the machines as an extension of their family and cultural values and in return for a donation of food or a glass of beer, these immigrants supported the political bosses with the expectation that they would give them a voice for the grievances. The growing popularity of the urban machine contributed to a growing tendency for American politics to be separated into two spheres: workplace concerns delegated to unions and community issues left to an electoral fate.

Urban bosses maintained their popularity by offering forms of public benevolence such as donations of food for Thanksgiving, giving jobs to the unemployed, appropriating funds for city improvement, and other forms of what might be called mass bribery. Although reformers protested these ways of gaining votes, claiming it was based on corruption, these political bosses were the only source of welfare that the urban poor had access to. Loyalty to the urban machine seemed to promise these people a road to social mobility, with success of the bosses seeming to promise personal success. Americans came to expect politics to address their everyday problems of living in poverty in poor living conditions in the cities. This was a time before formal welfare programs such as social security, unemployment insurance, and food stamps; the big bosses created a precedent for the political reform models that would follow.

As early as 1860, there was an elite minority whom were opposed to the political machine and instead organized under the the hope of achieving municipal reform. These civic reformers battled the political bosses by attempting to form their own version of an organized urban government. The political machine was a form of ward-based politics with the typical ward-elected representative being a modest worker who lived in the ward itself. Through this way, immigrants and their representatives gained ground in city councils which alarmed the elite who feared erosion of their authority. Business and professional leaders intervened in the political affairs and constituted reform leagues to restore order to American city politics. These reform associations campaigned for cuts in expenditures and tax rates, drafted legislation, and revised charters claiming that economic expansion would eventually help the working class. Such groups as the Committee of Seventy of New York offered reform candidates that overpowered the Tweed Ring in New York in 1871, followed by similar reform candidates ousting the bosses in other large cities.

By applying principles of business management to cities, the elite were able to reorganize cities to separate policy making from administration through either commission form or city manager form of government. During this time, the earliest form of government was used, city commission government. In this form of government, voters elect a commission of five to seven members that constitute the legislative body of the city. They are responsible for taxation, ordinances, and other general municipal functions. One commissioner is designated as mayor to preside over meetings and other individual commissioners are each assigned executive responsibly for specific aspect of municipal affairs such as public works or public safety. In this way, the legislative and executive branch functions are blended into the same body. Although this type of city government was once common in early America, it later switched to the council-manager form of government due to the perceived limitations of the commission form.

In other cities, municipal reforms planned to recapture political power by shifting authority from elected to appointed officials. This form of city manager government was based on new municipal charters that shifted authority to expert commissions and executive departments that were elected or appointed by a citywide constituency in favor of professional and business interests. Under this form, the elected governing body (city council or city commission) is responsible for the legislative functions of the city and in turn appoints a professional manager to act as CEO, providing professional management to administrative operations in the city. This concept of government was influenced by the Scientific Management movement, with the hope of ridding cities of the pervasive political machine from of government that abused the system. It was thought that the appointed manager was an impartial manager that could carry out administrative functions.

The goals of municipal reform were efforts to remove partisanship from politics and politics from government, establishing a citywide rather than ward-based political system. They proposed a system to give the majority of the representation to the city's elite. Although there were efforts to revoke immigrant voting rights, it was never feasible because universal white-male suffrage was already too deeply ingrained in American society. To combat this, the immigrant and African-

American political leaders were replaced with a city commission dominated by the white commercial elite. This new government was able to cut expenses by only providing services to wealthy white neighborhoods. This established upper-class political control and reshaped the boundaries between different races and classes more distinctly than ever before. To further combat the city bosses, reformers tried to institute citywide elections and nonpartisan ballots to take away the power from the ethnic neighborhoods. Thus, elite men of social standing were able to reclaim their office holding. To further downplay the impact of the city bosses, reformers created objective standards for hiring municipal employees, using written examinations rather than boss affiliation as the qualifying basis for city jobs.

City bosses were forced to conform with these reformers in the late nineteenth and early twentieth century, when these bosses saw the political advantages of supporting municipal reform with the public ownership of utilities and labor legislation that they hoped would help their constituents. With the blurring of municipal reformers and the big city bosses, the government shifted their focus from the business elite to the welfare of the working classes, bolstering relief agencies, authorizing public works for unemployment relief, and persuading merchants to keep prices low and not lay off workers. Several mayors of this time had a great impact on other reform mayors, urging cities to assume greater social responsibility and stressing the need for social justice and social inequality. These goals were believed to preserve what they thought was the American dream that was in sync with "American tradition". They sought to created a successful "clean government" which could match the functions that the political machines and city bosses had previously held. The reformers proposals was the notion that city government should strive to create a climate for economic growth through efficient administration. Although the municipal reformers succeeded in improving public administration by reducing corruption and providing public welfare services, they tended to view urban society only in moralistic and business terms and ignored many of the long-term social problems and provided an incomplete substitute for the previous welfare functions of the machine.

Beginning in 1870, reformers moved their interests from city reform to social reform. American socialists began to win political office by addressing the needs of the poor: urban inequality, poverty, and lack of welfare services. Because the political sphere was dominated by the elite white male class, both women and minority working-class turned their focus to reform association tactics with the goal of influencing political leaders. Reformers tried to secure legislation to address social problems by increasing the government's role in both social welfare and economic life. People began to come together to achieve this common goal of social reform. Before this time, the government had adopted a policy of laissez-faire, believing that the natural order of society ensured equilibrium and the government should not interfere with this natural order. However, this is what led to corruption by big city bosses and the reformers instead began to adopt a belief of community responsibility for promoting the welfare of everyone. This new idea challenged older notions of "survival of the fittest", that the economy and government was a matter of empowering only the best men of society. Agencies and commission seeking social reform sprung up in large urban cities and gave a new political voice to women, giving them somewhat of a political profession. As communication technologies continued to advance, the greater public began to examine exposes of the injustices of urban cities, creating ideas of personal, middle-class values of order and morality. Now, instead of believing in "survival of the fittest", social reformers adopted a structural cause explanation for the cause of poverty; that poverty was a direct result of environment rather than personal weakness. This was the beginning of what is now known as the Social Gospel movement.

Social Gospel emphasized the humane aspects of Christianity wherein the salvation of society should replace the salvation of an individual as the principal goal. Reformers sought salvation through good work and social betterment and worked to relieve the ills of society. Social Gospel reformers believed that they could restore order to society by reforming the environment and creating a moral groundwork. One of the ways they sought to do this was by creating institutional churches in low-income neighborhoods and closing down saloons, the center of the corruption of the former political bosses. By giving the working-class a moral basis and taking away the vice districts of the cities, reformers believed that most of society's problems would be remedied. Educational reform also became a basis for betterment of the poor. It was believed that educating immigrants and those in poverty would better assimilate them into society and provide them with a form of social mobility. However, this education only served to prove a further distinction between class and racial stratification by specifically training the children of immigrants and the poor for manual labor.

Settlement Houses, such as the Hull House founded by Jane Addams in 1889, opened by young, educated, religious, middle-class women with idealistic values served the interests of the poor in attempt to bridge the gap between classes. Settlement houses became the hub of reform in cities, acting as educational centers, information clearinghouses, and places of political debate. They backed housing reforms and regularity legislation to benefit both immigrants and other urban poor people.

This rise of urban liberalism in the progressive era relying on government intervention in society created labor and welfare reform, regulation of big business, and electoral reform. Official welfare programs were created in cities such as workman's compensation, widows' pensions, limited hours of labor, workplace safety regulations, and regulated tenement house housing. It was thought that regulation was the surest way of of stabilizing the city's economic conditions. This was the beginning of the combination of government and public interest, when political leaders finally took on social welfare as the top priority of the political agenda. Where the government was once dominated by an elite few, government began to open up to others to aid everyone's interests.

The progression of the United States government saw several forms of government in large urban cities. There are now five major types of types of municipal government found in cities and towns throughout the United States: Mayor-Council (Strong Mayor), Council-Manager, Commission, Town Meeting, and Representative Town Meeting. The oldest form of government, Commission form, currently exists in only 1% of American cities. In this form of government, voters elect a small commission to oversee municipal administration. Another current form of current city government, Strong-Mayor form, existing in 34% of American cities today, gives an elected mayor total administrative authority and a wide range of political independence with little public input. However, Abuses in these two forms and perceived limitations led to many cities adopting the Council-Manager form of local government wherein elected city counsels appoint a professional manager to oversee the city operations. This latter form of government is currently used in 55% of United States cities with its most popular use in cities with a population over 100,000. The lesser known forms of government, Town Meeting and Representative Town Meeting, are also used in a very small percentage of today's cities. Town Meeting form is thought to be the purest form of democracy, however it's used in only 5% of municipalities. Similar to this form of government is Representative Town Meeting form, however this is used to least, existing only in 1% of American cities. These forms of government are a culmination of American history and a direct result of the corruption that plagued politics for years from the creation of America as an independent nation through the Progressive Era. Although we are still far from a "clean government", the government that exists today is far superior to once was and the ideas of Jefferson and Hamilton have survived centuries as they are still in place today in all areas of municipal and national government.

Works Cited

Chudacoff, Howard P., Peter C. Baldwin, and Judith E. Smith. *The Evolution of American Urban Society*. Upper Saddle River, NJ: Prentice Hall, 2010. Print.

"Federalists vs. Anti-Federalists." *Dowell Middle School U.S. History*. N.p., n.d. Web. 26 Feb. 2015. <http://dmshistory8.weebly.com/federalists-vs-anti-federalists.html>.

"Forms of Municipal Government." *Forms of Municipal Government*. National League of Cities, 2013. Web. 26 Feb. 2015. <http://www.nlc.org/build-skills-and-networks/resources/cities-101/city-structures/forms-of-municipal- government>.

"Hamilton vs. Jefferson." *United States History - Hamilton vs. Jefferson*. N.p., n.d. Web. 26 Feb. 2015. <http://countrystudies.us/united-states/history-41.htm>.

"Jefferson versus Hamilton." *Teaching History.org, Home of the National History Education Clearinghouse*. N.p., n.d. Web. 26 Feb. 2015. <http://teachinghistory.org/history-content/ask-a-historian/24094>.

"The Progressive Era." *Digital History*. N.p., n.d. Web. 26 Feb. 2015. <http://www.digitalhistory.uh.edu/era.cfm?eraID=11&smtID=2>.

"Twentieth Century Revolutions." *Digital History*. N.p., n.d. Web. 26 Feb. 2015. <http://www.digitalhistory.uh.edu/disp_textbook.cfm?smtID=2&psid=3176>.

YOUR KNOWLEDGE HAS VALUE

- We will publish your bachelor's and master's thesis, essays and papers

- Your own eBook and book -
  sold worldwide in all relevant shops

- Earn money with each sale

Upload your text at www.GRIN.com
and publish for free